William B. Norman

Catalogue of the Collection of Works of Antique Art

William B. Norman

Catalogue of the Collection of Works of Antique Art

ISBN/EAN: 9783744646963

Printed in Europe, USA, Canada, Australia, Japan

Cover: Foto ©Thomas Meinert / pixelio.de

More available books at **www.hansebooks.com**

NO. 177. MUSIC RACK, MARIE ANTOINETTE. NO. 1430, SAN DONATO CATALOGUE.

CATALOGUE

——OF THE——

Collection of Works of Antique Art

——AND——

Thoroughly Authenticated Historical Relics,

BELONGING TO

ROBERT H. COLEMAN, ESQ.,

of Lebanon, Pennsylvania, and purchased for him by the famous Connoisseur and Art Critic, the late James Jackson Jarvis, to be sold at
auction, under the direction of Archibald Rogers, Esq., of
New York, at

THE FIFTH AVENUE AUCTION ROOMS,

238 Fifth Avenue,

Tuesday Afternoon, November 29th, 1892, at 2 o'clock,

——INCLUDING——

Many of the rare and precious objects from the San Donato sale,
comprising: Antique Tapestries, Embroideries, Cabinet Work,
Metal Work, Furniture from early Italian to the period of
the French Empire, a magnificent pair of Candelabra
in Malachite and Gilt Bronze with mosaics, Antique
Arms, Armor, etc., Antique Silverware and
Jewelers' Work in Gold and Silver Gilt.

Paintings by Claude Lorraine, Gaspard Poussin, Velturalli of Venice, and
others, and together with personal relics of Queen Marie Antoinette
of France, the Emperor Napoleon I. and his family.

WILLIAM B. NORMAN,

AUCTIONEER.

THE managers of the Fifth Avenue Auction Rooms take pleasure in presenting in this, what is perhaps the most remarkable collection of historical and artistic curiosities and relics which has yet been offered to the American collector at an auction sale in this city.

The collection consists of objects of art, in gold, silver and the various applications of high-class gilt work, upon the finest models of the present and past centuries ; of choice pieces of tapestry and embroidery, sculpture, wood-carving, pottery, marbles, paintings and antiques of every sort.

This collection is chiefly composed of objects purchased at the sale of the collection of the late Prince Demidoff, at the Palace of San Donato, by Mr. James Jackson Jarvis, the famous connoisseur and expert, at that time the representative of the United States at Florence, and largely added to by Mr. Jarvis, through purchases at Venice, Genoa, Rome, Naples, and in the western provinces of Europe. This special collection was formed by Mr. Jarvis for Mr. Robt. H. Coleman, of Lebanon, Pa., and is now being sold under the direction of Mr. Archibald Rogers, of New York.

During the many years through which Mr. Jarvis represented this country in the north of Italy, he became famous as a collector of the rarities and beautiful objects of antique art which were procurable at that time within the reach of his diplomatic station. His private collection, which was dispersed by a sale in this city, was one of treasures, and he assisted many of our collectors in forming a class of their collections which, without his assistance, would have been impossible to them. It may be said that the entire collection which is herewith presented to the public is really a part of the collection of Mr. James Jackson Jarvis, and that its guarantee may rest upon this fact.

It includes not only many fine objects of antique art in porcelain, metal work, wood-carving, armor and the like, but a great many relics of attested authenticity and of the greatest historical value, relating to the French Court of the eighteenth century, and to Queen Marie Antoinette ; and a unique collection of objects directly connected with Napoleon I. and his family, positively authenticated by documents and pedigrees to be found in the catalogue. There are also contained in it a number of objects associated with personages conspicuous in early Italian history.

The objects which proceed from the San Donato collection will be found so specified, together with their numbers in the catalogue of that sale.

NO. 96. LARGE RECTANGULAR TAPESTRY PANEL. NO. 42, SAN DONATO CATALOGUE.

CONDITIONS OF SALE.

The purchasers shall give their names and addresses, and shall also, *if required*, pay down a cash deposit or the whole of the purchase money ; in default of which payment, the lot or lots purchased by them shall be immediately put up again and resold.

All articles purchased shall be removed from these premises immediately upon the conclusion of the sale. All goods left upon the premises after the conclusion of the sale will be solely at the risk of the purchaser, and The Fifth Avenue Auction Rooms shall not be held responsible for any loss thereof or for any damage thereto.

Should a purchaser desire any goods bought by him to be resold, such goods must first be paid for in full. A commission (to be agreed upon) will be charged by The Fifth Avenue Auction Rooms upon such resale, but any loss or gain resulting therefrom will be for the account of the person ordering such resale.

Any complaint respecting this sale, or any of the goods purchased thereat, must be made in writing to the undersigned, within twenty-four hours after the close of this sale or it cannot be entertained.

The sale of any article will not be set aside on account of any error in the description of such article contained in this Catalogue; nor shall The Fifth Avenue Auction Rooms be deemed a warrantor of the correctness of any such description, or in any respect responsible therefor, unless it shall give an express warranty thereof in writing in addition to such description. All articles are exposed for public inspection, for one or more days preceding the sale, and are sold as they are, without recourse.

Should the purchaser fail or refuse to pay the purchase money in full, or to remove the goods purchased within twenty-four hours after the close of this sale, the money deposited in part payment shall, at the option of The Fifth Avenue Auction Rooms, be forfeited. All goods not so removed within twenty-four hours shall be resold at public or private sale, without further notice, and if the amount realized at such resale—after deducting the charges and expenses attending the same—shall not equal the amount for which said goods sell at this present sale, the purchaser at this present sale shall make good the deficiency. This condition, however, is without prejudice to the right of The Fifth Avenue Auction Rooms, at its option, to enforce the contract made at this present sale, without reselling the goods.

The Auctioneers will not be held liable for non-delivery of any article above the amount paid by purchaser for such article.

WM. B. NORMAN,
Auctioneer.

CATALOGUE.

1. Double-edged sword, antique, with scallop-shell guard to hilt.

2. Antique hunting sword, the blade engraved with scenes of the chase ; wooden handle and shell-shaped guard.

3. A long rapier, with brass guards and knobs to hilt ; antique.

4. Curiously shaped spear, with lance head and side points.

5. Spear, with leaf and crescent pattern head and tasseled staff.

6. Short broadsword, brass hilt with small shell-shaped guard, on the blade engraved figures of mounted warriors and inscription " Vivat Prince Eugenius," etc.

7. Small, open headed halberd, tasseled staff.

8. A long fighting rapier, with iron guard and wooden handle ; antique, Italian.

9. A short rapier, or hanger, with perforated guard and knob at hilt, chisseled at the base of the blade ; antique.

10. Double halberd, with spear top and spiked base, the handle covered with velvet.

11. Roman broadsword, the hilt terminated with a lion's head, and an inscription on the guard.

12. Two-edged sword, with brass cross guard, carved, handle covered with sharkskin, and terminated with a brass crown ; antique.

13. Antique sword, two-edged, with wooden handle.

15. Single-edged sword, with iron hilt and crescent-shaped guard ; old Italian.

16. Persian battle-axe, blade and handle of steel, with gold or copper arabesques, the panels of the socket of the axe being chiseled in bird and animal forms ; antique.

17. Long-headed spear.

18. Spear, with side prongs, tasseled staff.

19. Double-edged sword, wood grip, crescent-shaped guard ; old Spanish.

20. Iron buckler, with elaborate ornamentation ; old imitation of an antique model.

21. Iron helmet, with pointed or spiked boss, surrounded by fleurs de lys, beads, etc., in relief ; old imitation of a very antique model.

22. Old Venetian glass chalice, turquoise blue, the stem having a sea monster in amber, sprinkled with gold and enamelled.

23. A dolphin, in antique Venetian glass, pale sea-green color.

24. Antique Venetian cup, with green glass figuring in relief on body.

25. Antique Venetian glass goblet, with delicate handle and ring ornamentation on the bowl.

26. Antique Venetian glass flower vase, with the twisted stem in pale gold green.

27. Antique Venetian glass cup, with vertical stripes in white enamel.

28. Tall Venetian glass goblet, with ornaments and lions' heads shot with gold.

29. Old Venetian candlestick, blue and opalescent glass encircled with gold.

30. A dragon in old Venetian glass, in colors.

31. Antique Venetian glass, four swans, in white and colored enamel on a base of opalescent glass.

32. Fine old Venetian wine glass, the bowl supported by a sea serpent design in pale sea-green glass, enriched with gilding.

33. Old Venetian glass jar with bosses in gold glass, the body with parallel lines in relief.

34. Antique Venetian bottle with handle, the neck fluted in wavy lines, the glass delicately tinted in green.

35. Old Venetian glass flower vase, very graceful Greek form.

36. Flower vase, the body and base in opalescent glass, the stem representing a flower in colored glass and enamels ; old Venetian.

37. Antique Venetian glass flower pitcher, pale celadon, with ornaments in turquoise blue glass.

38. Antique Venetian wine glass, with ornamented stem.

39. Antique Venetian glass flower vase, ornamented in turquoise blue.

40. Antique Venetian wine goblet, white glass, with ornamented stem.

41. Antique Venetian jar, relieved with lines of white enamel and lions' heads in colored glass in relief.

42. Antique Venetian glass bowl, ornamented with lateral bands and interlacing lines in white enamel.

43. Antique Venetian glass pitcher, enameled and gilt and additionally decorated with painted coats-of-arms and supporting ornaments.

44. Very old Venetian bottle, ornamented with colored glass in relief, and showing traces of antique painting.

45. Small pitcher of black enamel richly sprinkled with gold on a green and deep blue ground.

46. Large beaker, with corrugated body, relieved with lions heads in relief and shot with gold ; old Venetian.

47. Small flower vase, enameled and gilt on a deep green ground.

48. Antique Venetian glass flower bottle, with handles in colored glass ; bottom damaged.

49. Antique Venetian bowl, the stem and handles shot with gold.

50. Antique Venetian glass beaker, with raised ornaments, shot with gold.

51. Stand in Venetian glass, on base four ducks in colored glass and enamel, supporting a shallow dish, in the centre of which is a swan in opal glass and enamel.

52. Antique Venetian glass cup, enamel and gilt ornament at rim, and painted figure and flower decorations in colors.

53. Antique Venetian plate, in delicate opalescent glass, enameled with band in enamel and gold.

54. Venetian glass bowl, with portrait of the Doge Grimiani and decorations in enamels and gold on blue ground, dated, 1595.

55. Small vase, in colored glass, enamels richly sprinkled with gold; old Venetian.

56. Small lacrymal, in amber glass, with ornamentation in colors ; old Venetian.

NO. 138.   MADONNA'S CROWN.   NO. 1318, SAN DONATO CATALOGUE.

57. Old Venetian flower vase, richly enameled on a green ground and sprinkled with gold.

58. Antique Venetian glass goblet, deep blue, relieved with white enamel and gold decoration.

59. Antique Venetian glass decanter, the body, neck and stopper enriched with enamels and gold.

60. Antique Venetian glass goblet, with decorations on the rim in enamels and gold.

61. Antique Venetian glass tazza, enameled in colors and richly gilt, bearing the arms of a ducal house in enamel and gold.

62. Large bowl, in blue Venetian glass, richly enameled in colors, painted and gilt.

63. Venetian glass pitcher, Amber fluted body.

64. Venetian glass flower vase, white, supported on twisted stem.

65. Enamel, on copper, snuff box, with gilt mounting; decorated with paintings in colors in the glaze on all sides, and with portrait of a lady on the inner lid. Eighteenth century.

66. Piece of embroidery on silk, with painting; Portuguese. Fifteenth century.

67. Piece of gold brocade in rich floral design.

68. Figure of a warrior, standing upright; painted on glass; sixteenth century; wooden frame.

69. Stiletto of Corsini de Medici, 1540, with the arms of the Medici family engraved on one side of the blade and the initials of Corsini on the other. The knife has a corrugated back and is hollow, serving as a sheath for a small and fine stiletto which the Duke used in executing his private assassinations. The stiletto is notched at the point for poison. The handle is of ivory, with fluted carving, mounted with silver. Attached to it is the silver chain for suspending the weapon at the waist and a clasp to fasten it to the belt, showing a head of Jupiter and the Medici arms in relief.

70. Scallop-shaped snuff box, inlaid with silver on copper ; upon the lid a representation of the abduction of Io by Jupiter, inlaid and gilt.

71. Ivory bon bon box, the lid carved and delicately ornamented in gold and color ; on the inside of the lid the portrait of a lady, in colors ; period of Louis XIV.

72. Antique iron key, elaborately wrought with figures.

73. An enamel of The Nativity, in grisaille. Italian work after the original picture by Leandro Bassano. No. 713 in San Donato catalogue.

74. Antique powder horn, with the Medici arms and flowers, birds, fish and serpent carved in high relief.

75. Antique powder horn, richly engraved.

76. Antique powder horn, elaborately engraved with scenes of the chase ; dated 1515.

77. Small powder horn, in bronze gilt, with figures of warriors chiseled on the side panels, and rich ornaments in relief ; signed L. and dated 1574.

78. Large plaque, with floral decoration in colors ; antique Italian imitation of a Moorish design.

79. Patent of nobility of the brothers Sassi of Florence, issued by the Emperor Francis Joseph of Austria at Vienna in 1756 ; engrossed in fine script, relieved with gold, with the imperial arms duplicated in colors, on parchment. To this is attached, in a gilt bronze box, an impression of the great seal of the empire struck in red wax ; the obverse and reverse of the box bearing a coat of arms and an imperial trophy of arms, in rich chiseling, and the inscription " Deo et Imperio."

80. Pair of candlesticks, in gilt bronze, representing the stem of a flower, to which are attached leaves in green glass, relieved with gold, the sconce setting in a full bloom tulip in glass enamel.

81. Majolica inkstand, decorated in blue and yellow, with three wells. Italian.

82. Small Dutch Cabinet in ebony, of the XVIIth century, with eight compartments in turned ebony, upon each of which is painted a view of a city; the two doors representing on the inside the pictures of a Frisian man and woman standing, surrounded by a framework of ebony. No. 891 in San Donato Catalogue.

83. A picture in silk tapestry, representing a rural scene. Flemish work, seventeenth century, in a wooden frame. No. 1770, San Donato Catalogue.

84. Flat box or travelling casket, ebony, interlaid with an elaborate interlacing floral design in ivory, relieved with etching; upon the lid the lions of Tuscany; the inner side of the lid inlaid with a floral design in ivory; hinged with forged metal, and with handles of chiseled steel. Once the property of the Grand Duke of Tuscany.

85. Very elegant lady's cabinet, by Cressant, cabinetmaker to the Prince Regent of France, in rosewood, with beautiful ornamentation in marqueterie and gilt bronze of flowers, etc., and of the most graceful form of the period, which was the first half of the Eighteenth Century, the front made to lower, with four interior drawers. No. 1538 in San Donato Catalogue.

86. Louis XIV clock in gilt brass, with glass at front, sides and back, elaborate floral design, with colored inlays, the dial of brass, with the hours marked in blue on panels of white enamel. French. Eighteenth Century. With bracket and cover surrounded by figure.

87. Antique Italian casket, showing remains of color and gilding on engraved ivory on figure designs. The sides are paneled in pieces of ivory preserving the natural curve of the tusk, and present a unique and picturesque effect. The lid is relieved with bands of inlaying in stained ivory.

88. Bronze figure of a bacchante, who dances, holding a bunch of grapes in her hand.

89. Bronze figure of a fawn drinking wine from a sack.

18

90. Pair of candlesticks in bronze, with gilt inlays on reliefs, and sea-horses forming the handles.

91. Persian casket, brass, elaborately decorated and perforated.

92. Set of brass fire-dogs ; old Italian, with elaborate ornamentation, the bases supported by crowned hydras ; extremely rare and fine style of Italian metallic art.

93. A Persian salver, brass, with elaborate incised design.

94. Kneeling cloth, for a prie-dieu, in pale green velvet, with a lining of white satin, ornamented with an alternating embroidery of fleur-de-lys and of stars in gold ; this beautiful tapestry in perfect preservation belonged to the private apartments of Queen Marie Antoinette at the Petit Trianon and was used by her in kneeling at private worship. No. 896, San Donato Catalogue.

95. Table cover, in blue Genoese velvet, studded with gold, bordered with fringe and ribbon knots in gold. No. 849 in San Donato Catalogue.

96. Large rectangular tapestry panel, in purple velvet, magnificently decorated with an application of embroidery in gold and silver, presenting an interlaced floral design, which encloses in the centre a panel decorated with a vase, surrounded by horns of plenty. No. 42 in San Donato Catalogue.

97. Perfume burner, in Chinese cloisonne, with three feet and two S-shaped handles, decorated in arabesque designs in colored enamels on a turquoise ground. The knob of the cover is in bronze, chiseled and gilt, in the form of a dragon. No. 1657, San Donato Catalogue.

98. A large flat tazzo of malachite, mounted in gilt, in the pure Empire style.

99. Bellows. The panels elaborately carved in walnut wood in high relief, the design being continued on the nozzle ; stamped leather sides. Sixteenth Century work.

14

NO. 142.   SILVER TEA BOX.   NO. 1324, SAN DONATO CATALOGUE.

100. Carved ivory cane, once the property of Sigismund Malatesta, the tyrant of Rimini, 1460 ; the stick inlaid with ivory and the head showing carvings in high relief, with a portrait of Malatesta in a panel, the head in a morocco case.

101. Chinese vase, with rich landscape decorations in colors and gold.

102. Circular dish, with scene of return of warriors enclosed in border, figured in yellow and blue ; Italian majolica, Sixteenth Century.

103. An Ebony casket, with inlaid panels of ivory, etched in allegorical designs with many figures ; the top double-lidded, the lids hinged in the middle ; antique Italian.

104. Antique box with drawer, in ivory and ebony, the ivory elaborately pierced, with imperial double-headed eagle in ivory on top, and lion and horse in ivory on side panels.

105. Group in marble bronze of two young bacchants playing with a wine sack.

106. Two large baluster vases, in Chinese cloisonne enamel; the body decorated with flowers on a white quadrillated ground, with lambriquinated border ; the necks arabesqued with flowers on a green ground. No. 1649, San Donato Catalogue.

107. Large Sevres vase, in rich imperial green, relieved with decoration in gold and a vignette of the Departure of Achilles, with arms on which appear heads in relief in gold. A splendid and sumptuous piece of Empire work.

108. Pair of octagonal panels in carved wood ; in the centre in ovals surrounded by trophies of war, are sculptured in bas-relief the portraits of Two Potentates. Early Eighteenth Century.

109. Copper gilt hand bowl or vase, with stem, for holding perfumes ; decorated with repoussé and chasing : the lid surmounted by a small figure of Cupid. Russian work, Eighteenth century.

110. Gilt clock, Empire period, with balled feet and decorated

with swans and lyres standing on the base ; a figure of Diana playing the lyre, with a dog and weapons of the chase as supporters to the clock, which has a circular dial in white enamel.

111. Pair of candlesticks, Empire period, in gilt and bronze ; a female figure on a bee-hive base supports the branches for three candles.

112. Reclining figure of a Hermit in a landscape, painted on glass ; Venetian, Sixteenth Century ; wooden frame.

113. Limoge panel, enameled on copper, representing Venus standing erect, surrounded by animals ; oval picture in ebony frame, executed from a design by Raphael ; antique Italian.

114. Antique Florentine terra-cotta, representing St. John preaching, executed after a design by Andrea del Sarto; signed in initials and dated 1443, in a black frame.

115. A magnificent set of Venetian glass, consisting of an olive jar, beaker and dish, richly decorated in gold and enamels, formerly the property of the Doge Tiepolo (early Fourteenth Century) and bearing his arms. In a satin-lined case.

116. Vienna placque, modern, superbly decorated in colors and gold, with a central painting representing Guttenberg exhibiting to the burghers of Mayenne the first printed book in 1455 ; in a satin-lined case.

117. Play table, for backgammon, checkers and chess ; mahogany, with inlays of ivory and ebony, and decoration in gilt bronze of the purest empire style, with drawers for counters, chessmen, etc. ; a curious and beautiful piece.

118. Cabinet, Empire period, in San Domingo mahogany, with beautifully chiseled mountings in gilt bronze ; pilasters at sides of front, falling lid for writing, drawers and compartments inside, old steel lock and hand-forged key.

119. Table, mahogany, mounted with chiseled ornaments in gilt bronze, enclosing small panels of Sevres paste, with figures in relief in white on a blue ground ; the top with a raised rim of gilt bronze, and inlaid with remarkable beauty in the finest

French marqueterie of walnut on the mahogany ground. Finest Empire work.

120. Marble bust of Macchiavelli, showing the astute statesman posed upon the works on statesmanship and policy which he indited.

121. Circular bas-relief in marble, in square ebony frame ; representing three Satyr's heads ; designed in the vein of the school of Michael Angelo, with pans, pipes and bacchanal surroundings.

122. The Venus de Medici ; a fine copy of this famous antique statute in marble, size of the original.

123. "Cupid Blinding Venus"; a marble group representing the God of Love alighting on his mother's shoulders from behind and covering her eyes with his hands ; full of movement and spirit ; life size ; the work of the distinguished Italian sculptor, Barcaglia.

124. Part of a magnificent table service. The rims richly decorated with gold on a blue ground, with oval medallions in grisaille on a ground of gold ; the body of the pieces entirely occupied by paintings after celebrated pictures in the Belvidere Gallery in Vienna ; pieces of an exceptional quality of execution throughout. No. 540 in San Donato Catalogue.

125. Beautiful clock of the period of Louis XIV. in copper marqueterie, on red tortoise-shell, richly garnished with gilt bronzes, caryatides, canopy, masks, figures of Cupids and ornaments, surmounted by a statuette of Fame. No. 335 in San Donato Catalogue.

126. Perfume burner, with three feet and cover, in damasquened iron ; perforated ; very elegant in design, in the Oriental style ; by Zuloaga. No. 1626, San Donato Catalogue.

127. Bronze figure of a daring bacchant, by Le Quesne. Very spirited, in action and expression.

128. Group of the Farnese Bull, in colored or marble bronze.

17

129. Very fine Empire clock, in gilt ; a figure of Minerva seated and resting her right arm on a shield, upon whose oval face appears the dial of the clock ; on the base are laurel wreaths suspended on a spear. The makers of the clock, Chomire et Cie, Paris.

130. Pair of gilt candlesticks, in the form of fluted columns, with floriated capitals, each supporting four floriated branches ; fine examples of the Empire period.

131. Gilt vase, oval, with figures chiseled in relief on front and back, on a base ornamented with fine figuring. Empire period.

132. Circular terra-cotta in relief, showing Jove, his eagle at his feet, hurling thunderbolts, while his attendant cherubs blow storms through the clouds ; late Italian renaissance, in ebony frame.

133. Cabinet, Empire period, in San Domingo mahogany, simple but superbly chiseled gilt bronze mountings, falling lid, drawers inside ; antique locks and forged keys.

134. Pair of massive bronze door-knockers, from the Florescini Palace at Volterra, representing lions suspended from a large lion's head, and supporting a medallioned female head at the base. Sixteenth Century.

135. Large carved cabinet, in two parts ; the upper part glazed ; old oak, with column sculptured in figures, vine leaves, lions' heads and cherubims ; the lower part with four doors, ornamented with carved fruits ; attached to the central column is a lamp bracket. No. 1361 in San Donato Catalogue.

136. Set of fire dogs by the distinguished Italian sculptor Tacca, executed in colored or marble bronze. The base displays a female figure, supported by dragons and cupids, and the standards are ornamented with rams' heads and dancing forms, which support a figure of Cupid at the top. A most artistic and beautiful example.

18

NO. 147.   EXTREMELY RICH ALTAR CLOTH, XVI. CENTURY.   NO. 828, SAN DONATO CATALOGUE

137. Pair of large and beautiful Medici vases, in malachite,ornamented with bas-reliefs in gilt bronze of vine branches, figures, etc., resting on square pedestals displaying on each face a medallion of flowers in antique Florentine Mosaic ; with square bases of malachite, ornamented in the same manner ; the bronzes by Fenchère, surmounted by candelabra of 12 lights each, in gilt bronze, decorated with flowers and fruit. No. 311 in San Donato Catalogue.

138. Madonna's crown, in silver and silver gilt, sexagonal shape, each face representing the same subject in pierced work, with high points chiseled in figures and regal crowns ; the rods separating the panels with winged cherubs' heads and winged cherubs' heads suspended from each panel. No. 1318 in San Donato Catalogue.

139. Tankard, with handle and cover in silver-gilt, resting on three balled feet, surmounted by panels enclosing busts of Roman emperors ; in the centre a coat-of-arms, with the inscription "Johann Graue Elizabeth Berens, anno 1707 " ; on the cover a bas-relief of cupids and the inscription, " Wenn Lieb und Fried sich Küssen, wird unglück weichen Müssen," meaning, " When Love and Peace exchange a Kiss, Misfortune must its Power Miss." No. 1276 in San Donato Catalogue.

140. A circular bonbonniere, lined with gold, in blue enamel, relieved with pearls, with the eagle of France and the arms of Westphalia and Wurtemburg combined in gold, surrounded by the inscription," Firmness and Uprightness " ; this bon-bon box having been the property of the Queen of Westphalia, born the Princess Catherine of Wurtemburg. No. 198 in San Donato Catalogue.

141. Bracelet, formerly the property of the Queen of Westphalia, Princess of Wurtemburg, giving in an acrostic, formed by the initial of the name of each gem in it, the date of the Queen's birth ; also, in rose-diamonds, the initials C. J. (Catharine Jérome). The acrostic is formed by the French names of the gems to which we append their English titles :

19

N	Nacre—Mother of pearl.
E	Emerande—Emerald.
E	Emerande—Emerald.
L	Labrador—Labradorite.
E	Emerande—Emerald.
21	Date of the month, in rose diamonds.
F	Feldspath—Feldspar.
E	Emerande—Emerald.
V	Vermeille—Red stone, of the garnet species.
R	Rubis—Ruby.
I	Iris—Crystal.
E	Emerande—Emerald.
R	Rubis—Ruby.

The date of birth, 1783, is given in rose diamonds. No. 210 in San Donato Catalogue.

142. Silver tea-box, gilded in part, hexagonal in shape; the panels ornamented with busts of Roman emperors; the cover with a hinged handle, surrounded by a laurel wreath. No. 1324 in San Donato Catalogue.

143. Tankard of cylindrical form, with base and cover in chiselled and repoussé silver, decorated with flowers in relief; the handle in the form of a serpent; the lid, base, handle and interior gilded. German work of the middle of the Seventeenth Century. No. 1262 in San Donato Catalogue,

144. Antique silver-gilt chalice, ornamented in repoussé with flowers, fruits, animals and landscapes; the base and stern enriched with repoussé and chiseled work, and bearing pious inscriptions on two bands of the bowl. German Sixteenth Century work.

145. Handsome chassuble or priest's robe, in rich crimson antique Genoese velvet, with embroidered cross and band of the XVth century, representing the standing figures of eight saints, in, embroidery of colored silk on a gold ground; fine Florentine work. No. 425 in San Donato Catalogue

146. Superb chassable or priest's robe, in cherry satin, embroidered with flowers, birds, butterflies, and with floral relief in gold; in the centre a broad band in similar style, with the

Virgin embroidered in gold and silver. Florentine wo k of the XVIth Century. No. 428 in San Donato Catalogue.

147. Extremely rich altar cloth, in cloth of silver, with ornamentation of branches, vases, fruits, pomegranates, bunches of grapes, horns of plenty, and birds, embroidered in high relief in gold and silk, and richly fringed with gold. A sumptuous example of Spanish workmanship of the end of the XVIth Century. No. 828 in San Donato Catalogue.

148. Handsome chasuble or priest's robe, embroidered in gold, on heavy yellow silk.

PAINTINGS.

149

PAUL BRIL.

Born at Antwerp, 1554, died 1626 ; pupil of Daniel Voltermans, and first painted panels on furniture, etc. Visited Italy, and painted many devotional pictures for churches. In the latter part of his life devoted himself to small landscapes, painted mostly on copper, and esteemed for soft, sweet color.

THE PILGRIM.

In the foreground at the left, a poor pilgrim prays for power to resist temptation, at a wayside shrine. At the right the arch tempter, in the form of a hideous dragon, spits flame in the fury of disappointment at losing a victim. The background is a mountainous landscape, with a castle and monastery perched upon a craggy hill. Painted on copper.

150

ROBERT W. WEIR, N. A.

Born at New Rochelle, N. Y., 1803, died 1890. Studied in New York and Italy, became a National Academician in 1829, and in 1833 was made

21

professor of drawing at the United States Military Academy at West Point. His "Embarkation of the Pilgrims" is in the Capitol at Washington.

SCENE AT WEST POINT.

A view of the lower battery at West Point, and of the Hudson river, and the Highlands, taken from the summit of the hill. Signed at the left. Painted on millboard. /) ~ / (

151

LUDOLPH BACKHUYSEN.

Born at Embden, 1631, died 1709 ; pupil of Emerdingen and Dubbels. Ranked next to the younger Vandervelde as a painter of marine subjects, and in some of his works surpassed him.

MARINE.

At the right, in the foreground, an armed galliot is sailing towards a beach on which is a tall beacon. In the middle plane at the left is a majestic battle-ship under full sail. Other craft are seen in the background. Signed at the right. Painted on a panel, ' .

152

VETTURALI.

A native of Venice, where he was born and died in the Eighteenth Century. He adopted the same class of subjects as Canaletto, but painted with a warm and agreeable coloration and a style of his own, and was superior to Canaletto in his treatment of figures.

THE BUCENTAUR.

A scene on the Grand Canal, on the day when the Doge proceeds to perform the ceremony of marrying the city to the Adriatic. The Bucentaur or state barge is moored in front of the Ducal Palace. The canal is alive with gondolas and boats, and all the signs of a great fête day are visible. Painted on canvas. ')

NO. 158. COVERED TANKARD IN SILVER, GILT AND OXIDIZED.
NO. 1259, SAN DONATO CATALOGUE.

.

153

VETTURALI

L'ETE.

A summer festival in Venice. Gayly decorated gondolas and gorgeous barges enliven the canal, and splendidly dressed merry-makers emerge from the palaces to embark upon their errands of pleasure. Painted on canvas.

154

HOTCHKISS.

SCENE IN THE APPENINES.

A view from one of the higher elevations of the range of savage mountains which traverses Italy from north to south. On every side the grandeur and desolation of the magnificent solitude is revealed by gleams of sunlight through rifts in a clouded sky. Executed in a broad and powerful, and with strong and harmonious, color, on canvas.

155

GASPARD POUSSIN.

Born in Rome, 1613, died there 1675 ; pupil and follower of his cousin and brother-in-law, Nicolas Poussin, whose name he adopted. He painted pictures of the same class as Nicolas, but in a style of his own, characterized by strong drawing, vigorous action, and a fine feeling for color.

LANDSCAPE.

In the foreground at the left some boys are bathing at a fountain in a park which surrounds a ruined villa. In the centre two boys are killing a serpent with stones. At the right, in the middle ground, are seen the buildings of a village or town, and the same is presented under the mellow illumination of late afternoon. Painted on canvas.

23

CLAUDE LORRAIN.

Claude Gellés, called Le Lorrain from the province in which he was born in 1600, died in Rome in 1682. In his magnificent art is to be found the foundation of the great school of landscape painting of the present day, in which Nature and not imagination was relied on as the guiding spirit of the painter. His works are among the priceless treasures of the great art museums of the world.

LANDSCAPE.

At the left in the foreground the ruins of an ancient castle are seen on an elevation, above a grove of trees, under which some sheep are grazing. A little stream emerges into the foreground at the right, falling over a ledge of rock, and on the farther bank are trees rich in foliage. The distance in the centre shows a vast prospect of Italian landscape, terminated by hills, and the warm glow of a golden sunset pervades the picture, which is believed to have been executed about 1651. Painted on canvas.

---

157. Flemish tapestry, a noble piece in perfect condition, of the Sixteenth Century. The border shows a broad band elaborately ornamented with figures, fruits, flowers, etc., and bearing inscriptions in Latin. On the centre field is represented the diversions of a king ; the monarch seated in his park listening to a musical concert performed by maidens; while, in the background, knights hold a tournament in front of his palace ; lovers ramble in the wood, a huntsman departs for the chase, etc. An extremely rare and precious example, in a very convenient size, 11 ft. in height by 14 ft. in length.

158. Covered tankard in silver, gilt and oxidized, cylindrical shape, with the body ornamented with figures of fighting warriors ; on the cover the Lion of Haarlem rampant ; the handle ornamented with the figure of a siren in cariatide form ; elaborate floral decoration throughout and heads of cherubim on rim of cover ; Dutch work. No. 1259 in San Donato Catalogue.

159. Russian vase, chalice-shaped, in silver-gilt, with three applied medallions showing portraits of Peter the Great, Catherine, and Alexis ; the Russian eagle and two inscriptions ; the cover and base with medalions and branch-work, added in applique ; native work of the middle of the XVIIIth Century. No. 1255 in San Donato Catalogue.

160. Capo-di-Monte box, of rectangular form, decorated on cover and sides with mythological subjects in relief ; mounted in gilt bronze, of bamboo pattern, with four rosetted feet in gilt bronze. No. 1642 in San Donato Catalogue.

161. Splendid tankard, in silver and gilt ; on the cover a swan ; standing on three feet formed like fruit ; the body decorated with figures of a bacchanal in high relief, and the handle modeled with a dog's head ; Dutch work, signed " H. Swan-E. Ertman, 1705." No. 1286 in San Donato Catalogue.

162. Tankard, on three-balled feet, in silver gilt; a medallion of Peter the Great on the cover ; on the body an Old Testament scene ; Russian work of the XVIIIth Century. No. 1297 in San Donato Catalogue.

163. A sculptured chimney-piece in rose ; antique marble, from the studio of the painter Fortuny. This artist, who was a famous collector of rare and beautiful pieces, left a great collection at his death, which was dispersed by public sale, Prince Demidoff purchasing a number for his San Donato collection. Letter E, San Donato Catalogue.

164. A Persian incense-burner, in brass, with enameling : globular form, supported on three feet.

165. Three Ribbons, respectively, of the Legion of Honor, the Reunion, and the Iron Crown ; these decorations, which had been regularly worn by the Emperor Napoleon I, were presented. by him to his brother, Prince Jerome Bonaparte, King of Westphalia, who gave them to his daughter, the Princess Mathilde, as a marriage gift. No. 205 in San Donato Catalogue.

166. Napoleon's Table Set: a silver spoon, with the Imperial Arms in relief ; a silver knife, engraved with the Imperial Arms, the blade by Grangeret, of Paris ; a coffee spoon in silver, with the Imperial Arms engraved ; a silver fork, bearing the Imperial Arms in engraving. All once the property of and used by the Emperor Napoleon I. at St. Helena. Nos. 185, 186, 187–189, San Donato Catalogue.

167. Autographic certification of General the Count of Montholon, that the above pieces were presented by the Emperor at St. Helena, September 30th, 1820, to M. Gentilini, who had been employed in his service as a souvenir upon Gentilini's quitting the island ; has Marshal Montholon's private seal attached. No. 190, San Donato Catalogue.

168. Report addressed to General Bonaparte, Commander-in-Chief, dated Cairo, 18th Messidor, year VII of the Republic, by Generals Bessiere, Duvivier and Lafou-Blaniac, whose signatures it bears ; and forwarded, with a signed postscript, by Bonaparte to General of Division Dugua, Inspector of Cavalry No. 257 in San Donato Catalogue.

169. A Sevres vase, decorated in gold and green on a white ground, and relieved by two panels in colors, representing respectively Napoleon I in his coronation robes as Emperor, and the Imperial Arms ; on a lapis lazuli base.

170. Gilt bronze fender, with warlike trophies, used by Napoleon I at his house during his exile at the Island of Elba.

171. Gilt bronze stand, with tongs and shovel in steel and gilt, belonging to the above set.

172. Twelve chairs, in carved wood, gilt, of the time of the Empire, upholstered in poult de soie, with gold studs, woven with clusters of fruit, flowers and garlands ; the framework of these chairs was originally the property of the Emperor Napoleon I. No. 144 in San Donato Catalogue.

173. A settee, in gilt wood, the backed arched, with the Imperial winged eagle displayed in a wreath of laurel ; upholstered

in garnet damask ; part of a suit once the property of the Emperor Napoleon I.   No. 1082 in San Donato Catalogue.

174. Marriage coffer, Florentine work of the Sixteenth Century ; heavily carved in gilt wood, resting on lion's-claw feet, the lid with an indented Byzantine design under the gold ; on the front panel the Judgment of Paris and a Wedding Feast, with the arrival of guests, painted in colors ; the end panels painted, representing respectively a young lover and his sweetheart, and a young wife ruling her old husband.   Made to hold the trousseau of a bride of noble family.

175. Large writing case, in gold and silver gilt, with all necessaries, given in 1810 by the Queen of Westphalia to her husband, Jérôme Bonaparte ; the case in walnut wood, externally ornamented with decorations in steel, set off with eagles and head in gold, and the initials J. N. with the royal crown ; the interior furnished with secret compartments.   This necessary contains :

An inkstand, in silver gilt ; a sand box ; two wafer boxes ; two paper presses, in steel, surmounted by a lion ; two candle holders ; a pounce bottle ; a bell surmounted by the imperial eagle ; a seal with the arms of Westphalia ; a seal with allegorical figures, and a pearl handle ; a pearl handled punch ; a pied-de-roi in mother of pearl ; two compasses, one with spare points ; a pair of paper scissors ; a crayon holder in silver gilt ; a silver gilt paper cutter, pearl handled ; a pearl handled scraper ; a pearl handled pen knife ; a pearl handled ruling pen ; a flat ruler, in ebony ; a squared ruler, encrusted with gold ; a lamp mounted in copper ; a steel point for opening the secret compartments ; nine watch key barrels ; a small key. No. 248 in San Donato Catalogue.

176. Two knives, fork and spoon, which belonged to Marie Antoinette ; one of the knives is gold and one steel, and both have tortoise-shell handles, decorated with gold bands and flowers.   The fork and spoon are gold, the handles decorated with Fleurs de Lys and garlands of ivy ; enclosed in morocco box, on the top of which is the initial A, surmounted by a crown.

177. Charming music rack, in hand-forged and repoussé iron work, designed by Louis XVI. of France, while he was still the Dauphin, as a present to his fiancée, Marie Antoinette of Austria. The design is of a decorative character, with a base supported at the ends by musical instruments, including a drum, Pan's-pipe, trumpets, tambourine and Breton bagpipe, from which springs floriated scrollwork supporting vases filled with royal lilies ; the centre being a lyre-shaped column, sustaining a medalion with the monogram of Marie Antoinette in roses, supported on either side by cupids, the composition completed by garlands of roses and the centre design supported at the base by Dolphins. This is an extremely interesting historical relic, not only as concerns its association with the artisan King and his hapless queen, but also as evidencing the natural talents which Louis XVI. possessed for artistic work in metal. No. 1430, San Donato Catalogue.

www.ingramcontent.com/pod-product-compliance
Lightning Source LLC
Chambersburg PA
CBHW021550270326
41930CB00008B/1441